Initial Response

Oct '11

To Peter

with respect & admiration
for your own work!

Halve O?

Initial Response

An A–Z of haiku moments

by

Maeve O'Sullivan

Alba Publishing

Published by Alba Publishing,
P O Box 266, Uxbridge
UB9 5NX, United Kingdom
www.albapublishing.com

© 2011 Maeve O'Sullivan
All rights reserved
No part of this publication may be reproduced, stored in a retrieval system, or transmitted by any form or by any means electronic, mechanical, photocopying, recording or otherwise without the prior written permission of the copyright owners.

A catalogue record for this book is available from the British Library

ISBN-10: 0-9551254-3-X
ISBN-13: 978-0-9551254-3-0

Edited, designed and typeset by Kim Richardson
Cover image and drawings by John Parsons
Printed by Cahill Printers Ltd, Dublin, Ireland

10 9 8 7 6 5 4 3 2 1

Contents

ACKNOWLEDMENTS	8
A: AUTUMN	10
B: BIRDS & BLOSSOMS	12
C: CHILDREN	14
D: DEARLY DEPARTED	16
E: EATING	18
F: FATHER'S DEATH DAY	20
G: GRADUATIONS	22
H: HALF A YEAR OF MOONS	24
I: I LUV SPAIN	26
J: J'AIME PARIS	28
K: KERRY	30
L: LOOSE HAIKU	32
M: MUSIC	34
N: NURSING HOME	36
O: ON THE BEACH	38
P: POSTCARDS FROM HOLLYWOOD	40
Q: QUO VADIS?	42

R: Rain	44
S: Spring & Summer	46
T: Tunisia	50
U: Until Death Do Us Part	52
V: Venice, Trieste & Rome	54
W: Winter	56
X: Xmas & New Year	58
Y: A Yew Tree at Bouzincourt	60
Z: Zen / meditation	62
Biographies	64

In memory of my father,
Maurice O'Sullivan, 1924-2010

Acknowledgements

Grateful acknowledgement is due to the editors and publishers of the following journals in which most of the haiku in this book, or versions of them, first appeared: *Blithe Spirit, Journal of the British Haiku Society* (UK); *Brittle Star* (UK); *InCognito, Irish Literary Journal* (Ireland); *Haiku Ireland, Ireland's International Journal of Haiku* (Ireland); (Haiku) *Presence* (UK); *The Stinging Fly* (Ireland); *The Stony Thursday Book 2010* (Ireland).

Anthologies

'after meditation class' was published in *Path*, the 2003 BHS Members' Anthology.
'another cork pops' was published in *Light*, the 2006 British Haiku Society Members' Anthology.
'Basque flower market' appears in *seed packets: an anthology of flower haiku* (bottle rockets press, 2010, US).
'emerging through' was published in *Earth*, the 2009 British Haiku Society Members' Anthology.
'her bony back' is published in *evolution: The Red Moon Anthology of English-Language Haiku 2010* (Red Moon Press, 2011, US).
'summer wedding' was published in *Celebration*, the 2010 British Haiku Society Members' Anthology.
'third journey' was published as the opening verse ('hokku') of the *renku**, *The Labyrinth's Core*, in the Vol. 5, No. 4 (December 2007) issue of the *Simply Haiku* website, www.simplyhaiku.com.

ACKNOWLEDGEMENTS

'whistling in the rain' was published in *Storm*, the 2007 British Haiku Society Members' Anthology.

Some haiku in the 'Xmas & New Year' sequence appear in *Census, the Second Seven Towers Anthology* (Seven Towers Agency, 2009, Ireland).

*The *renku* (linked chain of verses) was composed in July 2007 as part of the summer workshop *Writing from Within: Haiku and the Spiritual Path*, led by Maeve O'Sullivan and Kim Richardson at the Anam Cara Writers' and Artists' Retreat in Beara in West Cork, Ireland.

Awards

'around the corner' was commended in the first International Haiku Contest of the Bulgarian Haiku Club, *Haiku and Music* (2006).

'her bony back' won first place in the Haiku Ireland Kukai No. 20 (online members' competition) in Spring 2010.

'I blow raspberries' won the Haiku Museum of Literature Award for Vol. 20 No. 4 of *Blithe Spirit* (December 2010, UK).

Note: 50% of the profits from this book will go to the charity Rokpa UK towards projects in Tibetan areas of China.

Autumn

September sunrise
seagulls strolling
across the empty pitch

by the stone crucifix
bursting with red berries—
cotoneaster

nothing left
of yesterday's blackberries
this invisible thorn

Autumn

riverside woodland
autumn leaves resting
on a dry waterfall

childhood swing
long gone from here—
wild mushrooms

leaving Bull Island...
the plaintive cry
of unseen sandpipers

Birds & Blossoms

snowdrop bulbs
a seagull wheels overhead
sends out a long cry

busy afternoon
a glance outside
magnolia flowering

hard to tell
the blossom from the butterfly
this May afternoon

Birds & Blossoms

prize-winning poem—
wagtails move in low arcs
towards the podium

waxing moon—
flying across the waterfall
lone magpie

cornflowers
in this wild garden
two city eyes

Children

six months pregnant
she sizes up the new prams
with disbelief

I blow raspberries
into your tiny palm—
sleepy nephew

twins' birthday party
their mother gives her
half a hug

Children

photo of his son—
he brushes a speck of dust
off the left cheekbone

a young girl
smoothes her mother's hair back
outpatients

my friend's eight-year-old
asks me quietly
if I have children

Dearly Departed

old man coughing
newspaper open beside him—
death notices

news of her death—
stepping aside
to let the buggy pass

applause for the deceased
lasting
from the altar to the church door

Dearly Departed

thunderous applause
and a standing ovation
for the dead showman

suicide burial
robin song getting louder
as he's laid to rest

he poses
on his burial plot
chats about his 'neighbour'

Eating

at the salad bar
one man, one woman
apple on the side, untouched

conversation
interrupted, a plate smashing—
asparagus tips

one hundred degrees
ice-cold lemonade
warm banana bread

Eating

Pancake Tuesday
drips of honey
on the restaurant review

silent meal...
we drink our wine
at the same rate

coffees after lunch
he picks out
a heart-shaped chocolate

Father's Death Day

father's death day
after hours of phone calls
soft November rain

one sixth of his weight
snug
on my left shoulder

a week since his death
shaking the heavy duvet
into its cover

Father's Death Day

graduation night
wiping the dirt from his grave
off my good black boots

after five weeks
of condolences—
first Christmas card

midnight arrives...
ringing in the first
fatherless year

Graduation

fully-fledged robin
admiring his reflection—
graduation day

graduation night:
short skirts, high heels
the sound of sirens

visiting graduates
hesitate
to enter the staffroom

Half a Year of Moons

pink moon hiding—
a police helicopter
shines its searchlight

blossom moon...
baking bread
for tomorrow's goodbye

after the barbeque
strawberry moon
over Dublin Bay

Note: In North American Indian folklore, the full moon of each month is given a name.

Half a Year of Moons

coastal road trip:
heading south
towards the straw moon

last night
of our retreat...
corn moon-viewing

harvest moon—
finding the house key
I no longer use

cathedral market
smells of incense and leather—
I buy a choker

Basque flower market
an orange hibiscus
trumpets its presence

waiting for the bus...
several stemfuls
of cherry heaven

I Luv Spain

on the back of this coin
the famous cathedral
I visited today

full moon, fiesta
dancing on the beach—
shadows of palm trees

back by the Liffey
shells from Chipiona strand
jangle in my bag

J'Aime Paris

plane to Paris
I search for the seat belt,
find a toy soldier

the water is still
a boy watches—
did someone turn the fountain off?

October sunshine
the guitar player rests—
Pont des Arts

J'Aime Paris

gallery visitors
photograph the paintings
without looking

airport building
besieged by hailstones—
Bastille Day

on my return home
a sunflower:
just like the one in the Metro

Kerry

something moving
uphill through the bluebells:
cotton-tail

two thousand acres
of Lough Currane—
mosquitos on the windscreen

castle ramparts
bird's eye view
of swallows wind-reaping

Kerry

over the nettles
the white butterfly
your cat loves to punch

August sunshine
wigwams of turf sods—
final cut

sandpipers graze
then take off as one...
South Kerry sunset

Loose Haiku

Sunday morning
radio voices chattering
a tulip petal falls…

stained-glass ceiling
wobbling
in my coffee cup

following me
the matchmaker's eyes
in the photograph

Loose Haiku

a giant bee
flies by the old man
embroidering…

wondering
what it was all week:
hornbeam tree

at the pier's end
an upturned bell
the silent foghorn

MUSIC

solo banjo
silencing the session
with a new tune

midway through the lament
opening my eyes
to see hers closed

temporarily
off-duty, the conductor
swaying to a jig

Music

youth orchestra
ringless fingers
rendering Rossini

around the corner
from the Dvořák Museum
a drummer practising

flute notes evoking
I Am Sleeping
Do Not Wake Me

Nursing Home

a single strand of tinsel
wrapped around her bedrail:
Christmas Eve

slowly she peels
the easy-peel orange—
afternoon visit

her bony back
against my palm—
Mother's Day

Nursing Home

rain-filled Monday
nursing home residents
sing *Que Será, Será*

once again covering
my Mum's hand with his—
this stranger

a difficult visit
her wheelchair tyres
deflated

On the Beach

Barbie at the beach
miniature ghetto-blaster
silent beside her

a handsome couple
jumping over the waves—
their naked daughter

a rescue helicopter
whirring overhead—
jellyfish on the sand

On the Beach

three horses sea-swimming
spotted just as
the film runs out

Ballyheigue beach
a small group circles
the dead dolphin

sinking August sun
on Inch Strand
last ice-cream

photograph
"how did you meet your friend?"
fingerprints

wafting
through the kitchen screen door—
smell of a skunk

drying the pink
a small fan at my feet:
nail station

Japanese Garden
a strong sweet scent—
we search for the flower

Cha Cha Lounge
slumped over the counter—
the bartender

open-air screening
we pause the movie—
coyotes howl

Quo Vadis?

rush hour traffic
a boy on the bus
reading *On The Road*

almost-collision
bus driver brakes just in time—
passengers applaud

approaching the bus stop
our hoods go up
their umbrellas down

Quo Vadis

Good Friday
the rustle of newspapers
on the train journey south

platform—
is that my man
in the spring sun?

summer night breeze
even the trains
have gone to bed

Rain

between orange sky
and diagonal rain
my friend the heron

whistling in the rain
the cyclist too is
whistling in the rain

her umbrella blows
inside out again—
mother laughing

Spring

emerging through
a gravelled garden
daffodil shoot

a twig skidding
across the pond's surface—
February afternoon

gorse flowers
cutting through their sweet smell
birdsong

Spring

behind the willow curtain
the pen builds her nest
twig by twig

birdsong
punctuated by dialogue—
ewes and lambs

long ladder leaning
against a fruitless tree—
spring sunshine

Summer

first rain
a red blush appears
on the strawberry

third journey
to the labyrinth's core—
the sun breaks through

dodging clouds
and Manhattan skyscrapers –
June blue moon

Summer

late afternoon sun
my voice, my parents' voices
singing *Summertime*

a pause
in the discussion—
soft summer rain

late summer sunshine
filtering through
the heart-shaped bower

Tunisia

at the wadi
bridge half-built by Germans
a toy car rolls down the bus

Sahara sunset
the dromedaries' shadows,
legs even longer

fossils packed in
so closely together
where does shell end & rock start?

Tunisia

a tiny brown frog
leaps from the spring pool
back into camouflage

Holy City market
hawkers ignore
the call to prayer

last leg of the journey
a young camel waits
outside the slaughterhouse

Until Death Us Do Part

drying the champagne glasses
I smile again
at the good news

we place the golden beads
carefully
onto her sister's wedding cake

another cork pops—
between us and the town
red-windowed river boats

Until Death Us Do Part

summer wedding
women in cowboy hats
line-dancing to a jig

Chinese restaurant
the bride throws her bouquet
we collect our order

playing guitar
first time since the wedding
fingernails grown already

Venice, Trieste & Rome

I tell him I'm alone:
the look of horror
on the gondolier's face

tall sea pine,
please don't drop
your cones on me!

summer afternoon
sun on the Adriatic
this wartime bunker

Venice, Trieste & Rome

piazza-hopping
church-crawling
I stumble into a Mass

a bin truck
blocking my view of St. Peter's—
rosary beads up front

this morning's rain
drained off
inside the Pantheon

Winter

November morning
the rainbow follows me
all the way to work

slowly filling
black pepper grinder...
first snow

love all
untrammelled snow
these tennis courts

Winter

pedestrian lights
a girl in pink hat and shoes
dances herself warm

frosted branches
we zoom in
on the singing robin

hoarfrost melting—
droplets
on the dead badger's fur

Xmas & New Year

filling the house
with *Silent Night*:
uileann pipes

left inside the room
a party-goer's coat—
this freezing night!

Christmas Eve night
an empty taxi rank—
biting wind

Xmas & New Year

New Year's Eve
hot wax from the old candle
hardens in the bath water

just you & I
wind & bog
this New Year's Eve

midnight passes...
quietly, not embracing
we stand together

A Yew Tree in Bouzincourt

('REV D. V. O'SULLIVAN, CHAPLAIN TO THE FORCES',
killed giving last rites, July 1916)

    under the yew tree
    by the large crucifix:
    my great-uncle

    on his grave
    roses in bloom
    like in the old war song

    just five days
    after his anniversary
    soft rain falling

A Yew Tree in Bouzincourt

over the wall
a dozen rows
of soldiers' graves

a white butterfly
flits from stone to stone
birdsong

on the way home
we cross the wide Somme
slowly moving

Zen / Meditation

yoga movement
chimney pots coming into view
disappearing...

after meditation class
not recognising
my new black shoes

she stops reading
the question inside my head
disappears